THE MIND OF THE ENTREPRENEURS

10 steps toward starting your business, 2023.

By

Carl King

Copyright © January, 2023.

Editted by New life publishing press.

New york city.

All Right Reserved

No part of this book may be reproduced, transmitted in any form or by any means electronically, mechanically, photocopying, recording or otherwise without prior permission from the copyright owner.

1. CONDUCT A MARKET RESEARCH

Market research will let you know if there's a chance to transform your thought into an effective business. It's a method for social event data about expected clients and organizations previously working in your space. Utilize that data to track down an upper hand for your business.

USE STATISTICAL SURVEYING TO TRACK DOWN CLIENTS

Statistical surveying mixes customer conduct and financial patterns to affirm and further develop your business thought. It's significant to comprehend your buyer base all along. Statistical surveying allows you to lessen gambles even while your business is still a glimmer in your eye. Accumulate segment data to more readily comprehend valuable open doors and constraints for acquiring clients. This could remember populace information for age, riches, family, interests, or whatever else is pertinent for your business.

Then, at that point, answer the accompanying inquiries to get a capacity of your market:

Request: Is there a longing for your item or administration?

Market size: What number of individuals could be keen on your contribution?

Monetary markers: What is the pay reach and work rate?

Area: Where do your clients reside and where might your business at any point reach?

Market Immersion: What number of comparable choices are as of now accessible to customers?

Valuing: What do potential clients pay for these other options?

You'll likewise need to stay aware of the most recent independent company patterns. It's vital to acquire a feeling of the particular portion of the overall industry that will influence your benefits. You can do statistical surveying utilizing existing sources, or you can do the exploration yourself and go direct to buyers.

Existing sources can save you a great deal of significant investment, yet the data probably won't be as well defined for your crowd as you'd like. Use it to respond to questions that are both general and quantifiable, similar to industry patterns, socioeconomics, and family livelihoods. Check on the web or begin with our rundown of statistical surveying assets. Asking buyers yourself can give you a nuanced comprehension of your particular interest group. In any case, direct exploration can be tedious and costly. Use it to respond to inquiries concerning your particular business or clients, similar to responses to your logo, enhancements you could make to purchasing experience, and where clients could go rather than your business.

The following are a couple of strategies you can use to coordinate examination:

- Reviews
- Surveys
- Center gatherings
- Top-to-bottom meetings

Utilize serious examination to find a market advantage

The cutthroat examination assists you with gaining from organizations going after your expected clients. This is critical to characterizing an upper hand that makes a manageable income.

Your cutthroat examination ought to recognize your opposition to product offering or administration and market fragment. Evaluate the accompanying qualities of the cutthroat scene:

1. Piece of the pie
2. Qualities and shortcomings
3. Your open door to enter the market
4. The significance of your objective market to your rivals
5. Any boundaries that might ruin you as you enter the market
6. Roundabout or optional contenders who might affect your prosperity.

Free private company information and patterns

Numerous dependable sources give client and market data at no expense. Free measurements are promptly accessible to help forthcoming entrepreneurs.

2. WRITE YOUR BUSINESS PLAN

Your business plan or field-tested strategy is the underpinning of your business. It's a guide for how to design, run, and develop your new business. You'll utilize it to persuade individuals that working with you — or putting resources into your organization — is a savvy decision.

Marketable strategies assist you with maintaining your business

A decent field-tested strategy guides you through each phase of beginning and dealing with your business. You'll utilize your strategy as a guide for how to construct, run, and develop your new business. It's a method for thoroughly considering the vital components of your business. Marketable strategies can assist you with getting financing or welcoming new colleagues. Financial backers need to feel sure they'll see a profit from their venture. Your marketable strategy is the device you'll use to persuade individuals that working with you — or putting resources into your organization — is a brilliant decision.

Pick a strategy format that works for you

There's no correct method for composing a strategy. What's significant is that your arrangement addresses your issues. Most strategies can be categorized as one of two normal classifications: conventional or lean startup.

Customary marketable strategies are more normal, utilize a standard construction, and urge you to carefully describe the situation in each part. They will generally require more work forthright and can be many pages long. Learn new company plans are more uncommon yet at the same time utilize a standard construction. They center around summing up just the main places of the vital components of your arrangement. They can require just one hour to make and are ordinarily just a single page.

Conventional business plan

This sort of plan is extremely definite, finds the opportunity to compose, and is far-reaching. Banks and financial backers normally demand this arrangement.

Lean startup plan

This sort of plan is undeniably level of concentration, quick to compose, and contains key components as it were. A few loan specialists and financial backers might request more data.

Conventional strategy format

You could favor a conventional strategy design on the off chance that you're very meticulous, need a far-reaching plan, or plan to demand funding from customary sources. At the point when you compose your field-tested strategy, you don't need to adhere to the specific strategy frame. All things being equal, utilizing the areas that appear to be legit for your business and your necessities. Conventional marketable strategies utilize a blend of these nine segments.

Leader rundown

Momentarily let your peruser know your organization and why it will find lasting success. Incorporate your statement of purpose, your item or administration, and fundamental data about your organization's authority group, representatives, and area. You ought to likewise incorporate monetary data and significant-level development plans on the off chance that you intend to request funding.

Organization portrayal

Utilize your organization's portrayal to give itemized data about your organization. Carefully describe the issues your business addresses. Be explicit, and drill down the buyers, associations, or organizations your organization intends to serve. Make sense of the upper hands that will make your business a triumph. Are there specialists in your group? Have you tracked down the ideal area for your store? Your organization's depiction is the spot to flaunt your assets.

Market Examination

You'll require a decent comprehension of your industry standpoint and target market. Cutthroat exploration will show you what different organizations are doing and what their assets are. In your statistical surveying, search for patterns and subjects. What do fruitful contenders do? For what reason does it work? Could you at any point improve? This present time's the opportunity to respond to these inquiries.

Association and the board

Let your peruser know how your organization will be organized and who will run it.

Depict the lawful design of your business.

State whether you have or plan to integrate your business as a C or an S enterprise, structure a general or restricted association, or on the other hand if you're a sole owner or restricted obligation organization (LLC). Utilize a hierarchical diagram to lay out who's responsible for what in your organization. Show how every individual's interesting experience will add to the outcome of your endeavor. Consider including resumes and CVs of key colleagues.

Administration or product offering

Depict what you sell or what administration you offer. Make sense of how it helps your clients and what the item lifecycle resembles. Share your arrangements for protected innovation, similar to copyright or patent filings. On the off chance that you're doing innovative work for your administration or item, make sense of it exhaustively.

Marketing and sales

There's no single method for moving toward a showcasing procedure. Your methodology ought to develop and change to accommodate your special requirements. Your objective in this segment is to portray how you'll draw in and hold clients. You'll likewise portray how a deal will occur. You'll allude to this segment some other time when you make monetary projections, so try to portray your total promoting and deals methodologies completely.

Financing demand

Assuming you're requesting financing, this is where you'll frame your subsidizing necessities. You want to make sense of how much subsidizing you'll require over the following five years and why you'll utilize it. Indicate whether you need obligation or value, the terms you'd like applied, and the timeframe your solicitation will cover. Give a definite depiction of how you'll utilize your assets. Indicate on the off chance that you want assets to purchase hardware or materials, pay compensations, or cover explicit bills until income increments. Continuously incorporate a portrayal of your future vital monetary plans, such as taking care of obligations or selling your business.

Monetary projections

Supplement your subsidizing demand with monetary projections. You want to persuade the peruser that your business is steady and will be a monetary achievement.

Assuming that your business is now settled, incorporate pay explanations, asset reports, and income proclamations for the last three to five years. If you have other security you could set against a credit, try to show it now. Give a forthcoming monetary standpoint for the following five years. Incorporate guage pay explanations, monetary records, income articulations, and capital use financial plans. For the primary year, be much more unambiguous and utilize quarterly — or even month-to-month — projections. Make a point to make sense of your projections, and match them to your financing demands.

This is an incredible spot to utilize diagrams and outlines to recount the monetary story of your business.

Reference section or appendix

Utilize your reference section to give supporting archives or different materials that were exceptionally mentioned. Normal things to incorporate are records of loan repayment, resumes, item pictures, letters of reference, licenses, grants, licenses, authoritative reports, and different agreements.

Model conventional strategies

Before you compose your marketable strategy, read the accompanying model strategies composed by fictitious entrepreneurs. Rebecca possesses a counseling firm, and Andrew claims a toy organization.

Lean startup format

You could favor a lean startup design to make sense of or begin your business rapidly, your business is somewhat straightforward, or you plan to routinely change and refine your marketable strategy. Lean startup designs are diagrams that utilize just a small bunch of components to depict your organization's incentive, framework, clients, and funds. They're valuable for envisioning tradeoffs and principal realities about your organization. There are various ways of fostering a lean startup format. You can look through the web to track down free formats to fabricate your strategy. We examine nine parts of a model field-tested strategy here:

Key partnership

Note different organizations or administrations you'll work with to maintain your business. Contemplate providers, producers, subcontractors, and comparable key accomplices.

Key exercises

List the manners in which your business will acquire an upper hand. Feature things like selling direct to buyers, or utilizing innovation to take advantage of the sharing economy.

Distinct advantages

List any asset you'll use to make an incentive for your client. Your most significant resources could incorporate staff, capital, or protected innovation. Remember to use business assets that may be accessible to ladies, veterans, Local Americans, and HUBZone organizations.

Value proposition

Make an understood and convincing assertion about the exceptional worth your organization brings to the market.

Client connections

Portray how clients will interface with your business. Is it mechanized or individual? Face to face or on the web?

Thoroughly consider the client experience from beginning to end.

Client sections

Be explicit when you name your objective market. Your business will not be for everyone, so it's critical to have an unmistakable feeling of whom your business will serve.

Channels

List the main ways you'll converse with your clients. Most organizations utilize a blend of channels and enhance them over the long haul.

Cost structure

Will your organization center around decreasing expense or augmenting esteem? Characterize your system, then, at that point, list the main costs you'll confront seeking after it.

Income streams

Make sense of how your organization will bring in cash. A few models are immediate deals, participation expenses, and selling publicizing space. Assuming that your organization has various income streams, show them all.

Model lean field-tested strategy

Before you compose your field-tested strategy, read this model strategy composed by an imaginary entrepreneur, Andrew, who possesses a toy organization.

3. FUND YOUR BUSINESS

Your marketable strategy will assist you with sorting out how much cash you'll have to begin your business. On the off chance that you don't have that sum close by, you'll have to one or the other raise or get the capital. Luckily, there are more ways than at any time in recent memory to find the capital you want.

Decide how much financing you'll require

Each business has various necessities, and no monetary arrangement is one-size-fits-all. Your monetary circumstance and vision for your business will shape the monetary fate of your business. When you know how much startup subsidizing you'll require, now is the ideal time to sort out how you'll get it.

Fund your business yourself with self-subsidizing

Also called bootstrapping, self-subsidizing allows you to use your monetary assets to help your business. Self-financing can come through going to loved ones for capital, utilizing your investment accounts, or in any event, taking advantage of your 401(k). With self-subsidizing, you hold unlimited authority over the business, however, you likewise face all the gambling challenges. Be mindful so as not to spend beyond what you can manage, and be particularly cautious if you decide to take advantage of retirement accounts early. You could have to deal with costly charges or damages, or harm your capacity to resign on time — so you ought to check with your arrangement's director and an individual monetary counselor first.

Get venture capital from investors

Financial backers can give you subsidizing to begin your business as funding speculations. Funding is ordinarily presented in return for a proprietorship offer and a dynamic job in the company. Small Business Organization

Funding contrasts with customary support in various significant ways. **Funding ordinarily:**

- ★ Concentrates high-development organizations
- ★ Puts capital as a trade-off for value, as opposed to obligation (it's anything but a credit)
- ★ Faces higher challenges in return for expected more significant yields
- ★ Has a more drawn-out venture skyline than conventional funding

Practically all financial speculators will, at least, need a seat on the governing body. So be ready to surrender a few pieces of both control and responsibility for the organization in return for financing.

Instructions to get investment financing

There's no dependable method for getting funding, however, the cycle by and large keeps a guideline request of fundamental stages.

Track down a financial backer or investor

Search for individual investors— in some cases called "private supporters" — or funding firms. Make certain to can sufficient foundation exploration to say whether the financial backer is respectable and has experience working with new businesses.

Share your marketable strategy

The financial backer will audit your field-tested strategy to ensure it meets its effective money management models. Most venture subsidies focus on an industry, geographic region, or phase of business improvement.

Go through the expected level of effort survey

The financial backers will take a gander at your organization's supervisory crew, market, items and administrations, corporate administration records, and budget summaries.

Sort out the terms

To contribute, the subsequent stage is to settle on a term sheet that portrays the agreements for the asset to make a speculation.

Speculation

When you settle on a term sheet, you can get the speculation! When an endeavor reserve has contributed, it turns out to be effectively engaged with the organization. Adventure reserves ordinarily come in "adjusts." As the organization meets achievements, further adjustments of support are made accessible, with changes in cost as the organization executes its arrangement.

Use crowdfunding to finance your business

Crowdfunding raises assets for a business from an enormous number of individuals, called crowdfunders. Crowdfunders aren't financial backers, since they don't get a portion of possession in the business and don't anticipate a monetary profit from their cash.

All things considered, crowd funders hope to get a "gift" from your organization as gratitude for their commitment. Frequently, that gift is the item you intend to sell or other unique advantages, such as meeting the entrepreneur or getting their name in the credits. This makes crowdfunding a well-known choice for individuals who need to deliver inventive works (like a narrative), or an actual item (like a cutting-edge cooler).

Crowdfunding is additionally well known because it's exceptionally generally safe for entrepreneurs. Besides the fact that you get to hold full control of your organization, assuming your arrangement comes up short, you're commonly under no commitment to reimburse your crowdfunders. Each crowdfunding stage is unique, so make a point to peruse the fine print and grasp your full monetary and legitimate commitments.

Get a private company credit (loan)

To hold unlimited oversight of your business, however, need more assets to begin, consider a private company credit. To expand your possibilities of getting credit, you ought to have a field-tested strategy, cost sheet, and monetary projections for the following five years. These devices will provide you with a thought of the amount you'll have to request and will assist the manager of an account with realizing they're pursuing a brilliant decision by giving you a credit. When you have your materials prepared, contact banks and credit associations to demand credit. You'll need to contrast offers to get the most ideal terms for your advance.

4. PICK YOUR BUSINESS LOCATION

Your business area is perhaps the main choice you'll make. Whether you're setting up a physical business or sending off a web-based store, the decisions could influence your expenses, lawful necessities, and income. Your business area decides the expenses, drafting regulations, and guidelines your business will be dependent upon. You'll have to settle on an essential conclusion about which state, city, and neighborhood you decide to begin your business in.

Research the best place to locate your business

You'll have to enroll your business, settle burdens, and get licenses and allows in the spot you decide to find your business. Where you find your business depends to some extent on the area of your objective market, colleagues, and your inclinations. Likewise, you ought to think about the expenses, advantages, and limitations of various government organizations.

Area explicit operational expense

At the point when you ascertain your startup costs, consider how various costs could cost pretty much relying upon your area. Costs that can differ essentially by area incorporate standard compensations, the lowest pay permitted by law regulations, property estimations, rental rates, business protection rates, utilities, and government licenses and charges.

Neighborhood drafting mandates

If you purchase, lease, fabricate, or plan to figure out an actual property for your business, ensure it adjusts to neighborhood drafting prerequisites. Neighborhoods are for the most part drafted for one or the other business or private use. Drafting statutes can confine or completely restrict explicit sorts of organizations from working in space. You could have fewer drafting limitations assuming you base your business out of your home, yet drafting mandates can in any case apply even to locally situated organizations. Drafting regulations are commonly controlled at the neighborhood level, so check with your division of city arranging, or comparative office, to learn about the drafting regulations in your space.

State and neighborhood charges

Consider the tax landscape for the state, province, and city. Annual expense, deals charge, local charge, and corporate duties can change altogether from one spot to another. A few states are notable for establishing charge conditions that are cordial to particular sorts of organizations. That is essential for the justification for why tech new companies, monetary organizations, and assembling will generally pack in a specific region of the country. Visit state and nearby government sites to figure out what the expense scene for your area seems to be. Your business area decides the charges, drafting regulations, and guidelines your business will be dependent upon. You'll have to settle on an essential conclusion about which state, city, and neighborhood you decide to begin your business in. Where you find your business depends to some extent on the area of your objective market, colleagues, and your inclinations. Moreover, you ought to think about the expenses, advantages, and limitations of various government organizations.

Locale explicit operational expense

At the point when you ascertain your startup costs, consider how various costs could cost pretty much relying upon your area. Costs that can differ essentially by area incorporate standard compensations, the lowest pay permitted by law regulations, property estimations, rental rates, business protection rates, utilities, and government licenses and charges.

Neighborhood drafting laws

If you purchase, lease, construct, or plan to resolve actual property for your business, ensure it adjusts to neighborhood drafting prerequisites. Neighborhoods are for the most part drafted for one or the other business or private use. Drafting laws can confine or completely prohibit explicit sorts of organizations from working in space. You could have fewer drafting limitations on the off chance that you base your business out of your home, however, drafting statutes can in any case apply even to locally situated organizations. Drafting regulations are normally controlled at the neighborhood level, so check with your branch of city arranging, or comparable office, to learn about the drafting regulations in your space.

State and nearby expenses

Consider the assessment scene for the state, area, and city. Personal duty, deals charge, local charge, and corporate assessments can change fundamentally from one spot to another.

A few states are notable for establishing charge conditions that are cordial to particular sorts of organizations. That is important for the justification for why tech new businesses, monetary organizations, and assembling will generally gather in a specific region of the country. Visit state and nearby government sites to figure out what the duty scene for your area seems to be.

State and nearby government impetuses

A few state and nearby legislatures offer extraordinary tax breaks for independent ventures. You could likewise find state-explicit private venture credits or other monetary motivating forces. Motivator projects and advantages are in many cases connected with work creation, energy productivity, metropolitan redevelopment, and innovation.

Federal government incentives

The central government offers advantages to private companies that agree with the public authority and are situated in underutilized regions. Look into the Generally Underutilized Business Zones (HUBZone) program to check whether you meet all requirements for particular admittance to government obtainment amazing open doors

5. PICK A BUSINESS STRUCTURE

The lawful design you decide for your business will affect your business enlistment necessities, the amount you cover in charges, and your own risk. The business structure you pick impacts everything from everyday tasks to charges, and the number of your resources are in danger. You ought to pick a business structure that provides you with the right equilibrium between legitimate securities and advantages. You'll have to pick a business structure before you register your business with the state. Most organizations will likewise have to get a duty ID number and document for the fitting licenses and allows.

Select cautiously. While you might switch over completely to an alternate business structure from now on, there might be limitations given your area. This could likewise bring about charge outcomes and accidental disintegration, among different difficulties.

Talking with business instructors, lawyers, and bookkeepers can demonstrate accommodating.

Audit normal business structures

Sole proprietorship

Sole proprietorship is not difficult to frame and gives you full oversight of your business. You're consequently viewed as sole proprietorship on the off chance that you carry on with work exercises however register as no other sort of business. Sole ownerships don't create a different business element. This implies your business resources and liabilities are not discrete from your resources and liabilities. You can be expected by and by to take responsibility for the obligations and commitments of the business. Sole owners are as yet ready to get a business trademark. It can likewise be difficult to fund-raise since you can't sell a stock, and banks are reluctant to loan to sole owners.

Sole proprietorship can be a decent decision for generally safe organizations and proprietors who need to test their business thoughts before framing a more conventional business.

Partnership

Partnership are the least difficult design for at least two individuals to claim a business together. There are two normal sorts of associations: Limited partnership (LP) and Limited liability partnerships (LLP). Restricted partnership have just a single general join force with limitless obligation, and any remaining accomplices have restricted responsibility. The accomplices with restricted obligation likewise will quite often have restricted command over the organization, which is recorded in an association understanding. Benefits are gone through individual government forms, and the general accomplice — the accomplice without limited liability — should likewise make good on independent work charges. Restricted risk associations are like restricted organizations, however, give restricted responsibility to each proprietor. An LLP shields each accomplice from obligations against the organization, they will not be liable for the activities of different accomplices.

Organizations can be a decent decision for organizations with various proprietors, proficient gatherings (like lawyers), and gatherings who need to test their business thought before framing a more conventional business.

Limited liability company(LLC)

An LLC allows you to exploit the advantages of both the enterprise and organization business structures.

LLCs shield you from individual obligations on many occasions, and your resources — like your vehicle, house, and investment accounts — will not be in danger on the off chance that your LLC faces liquidation or claims. Benefits and misfortunes can break went through to your pay without confronting corporate expenses. Notwithstanding, individuals from an LLC are viewed as independently employed and should pay independent work charge commitments towards Federal health care and Government managed retirement. LLCs can have a restricted life in many states. At the point when a part joins or leaves an LLC, a few states might require the LLC to be broken up and once again shaped with new enrollment — except if there's as of now an understanding set up inside the LLC for purchasing, selling, and moving proprietorship. LLCs can be a decent decision for medium-or higher-risk organizations, proprietors with critical individual resources that need to be safeguarded, and proprietors who need to pay a lower charge rate than they would with an enterprise.

Company

C corp

An enterprise, in some cases called a C corp, is a legitimate substance that is discrete from its proprietors. Companies can create a gain, be burdened, and can be expected legitimately to take responsibility.

Enterprises offer the most grounded security to their proprietors from individual responsibility, however, the expense to shape a company is higher than different designs. Enterprises likewise require greater record-keeping, functional cycles, and announcing.

In contrast to sole owners, organizations, and LLCs, companies pay a personal assessment of their benefits. At times, corporate benefits are burdened two times — first, when the organization creates a gain, and again when profits are paid to investors on their expense forms. Organizations have a free life separate from their investors. If an investor leaves the organization or sells their portions, the C corp can keep carrying on with work generally undisturbed.

Partnerships enjoy a benefit concerning raising capital since they can raise finances through the offer of stock, which can likewise be an advantage in drawing in representatives. Companies can be a decent decision for medium-or higher-risk organizations, those that need to fund-raise, and organizations that arrange to "open up to the world" or at last be sold.

S corp

An S enterprise, some of the time called an S corp, is an extraordinary kind of partnership that is intended to stay away from the twofold tax collection downside of normal C corps. S corps permit benefits, and a few misfortunes, to be gone through straightforwardly to proprietors' very own pay while never being dependent upon corporate expense rates. Not all states charge S corps similarly, however, most remember them the same way the national government does and charge the investors appropriately. A few states charge S corps on benefits over a predetermined breaking point and different states don't perceive the S corp political decision by any means, essentially regarding the business as a C corp.

S corps should document with the IRS to get S corp status, an alternate cycle from enrolling with their state.

There are extraordinary cutoff points on S corps. Look at the IRS site for qualification prerequisites. You'll in any case need to follow the severe documenting and functional cycles of a C corp.

S corps additionally have an autonomous life, very much like C corps. On the off chance that an investor leaves the organization or sells their portions, the S corp can keep carrying on with work generally undisturbed.

S corps can be a decent decision for organizations that would somehow or another be a C corp, but meet the models to record as an S corp.

B Corp

An advantage organization, some of the time called a B corp, is a for-benefit partnership perceived by a greater part of U.S. states. B Corps are not the same as C corps in reason, responsibility, and straightforwardness, yet aren't different by the way they're burdened. B corps are driven by both mission and benefit. Investors consider the organization responsible to create a public advantage notwithstanding a monetary benefit of some kind. A few states require B corps to submit yearly advantage reports that show their commitment to the public great. There are a few outsider B corp certificate administrations, yet none are expected for an organization to be lawfully viewed as a B corp in a state where the legitimate status is accessible.

Close corporation

Close partnerships look like B corps however have a less customary corporate design. These shed numerous customs that ordinarily oversee organizations and apply to more modest organizations. State rules change, however, shares are generally banned from the public exchange. Close enterprises can be controlled by a little gathering of investors without a directorate.

Non-profit corporation

Not-for-profit companies are coordinated to do noble causes, instruction, and strict, artistic, or logical work. Since their work helps general society, not-for-profits can get charged excluded status, meaning they don't pay state or government annual duties on any benefits it makes. Charities should record with the IRS to get charge exception, an alternate interaction from enlisting with their state. Philanthropic partnerships need to keep hierarchical guidelines the same as a normal C corp. They additionally need to adhere to exceptional guidelines about how they manage any benefits they procure. For instance, they can't disseminate benefits to individuals or political missions.

Philanthropies are frequently called 501(c)(3) partnerships — a reference to the segment of the Inner Income Code that is most normally used to concede charge-excluded status.

Corporative

A corporative is a business or association possessed by and worked to support those utilizing its administrations. Benefits and profit created by the helpful are dispersed among the individuals, otherwise called client proprietors. Commonly, a chosen governing body and officials run the helpful while customary individuals have to cast a ballot ability to control the course of the helpful. Individuals can turn out to be important for the helpful by buying shares, however how many offers they hold doesn't influence the heaviness of their vote.

Consolidate different business structures

Assignments like S corp and not-for-profit aren't on the up-and-up structures — they can likewise be perceived as an expense status. It's workable for an LLC to be burdened as a C corp, S corp, or a not-for-profit. These game plans are undeniably more uncommon and can be harder to set up. On the off chance that you're thinking about one of these non-standard designs, you ought to talk with a business guide or a lawyer to assist you with choosing.

Think about business structures

Think about the overall characteristics of these business structures, however, recall that possession rules, responsibilities, duties, and documenting necessities for every business design can fluctuate by state. The accompanying table is expected exclusively as a rule. If it's not too much trouble, meet with a business charge expert to affirm your particular business needs.

6. PICK YOUR BUSINESS NAME

Picking the ideal name is difficult. You'll need one that mirrors your image and catches your soul. You'll likewise need to ensure your business name isn't now being utilized by another person.

Register your business name to safeguard it

You'll need to pick a business name that mirrors your image and personality and doesn't conflict with the sorts of labor and products you offer. When you choose a name you like, you want to safeguard it. There are four unique ways of enlisting your business name. Every approach to enlisting your name fills an alternate need, and some might be legitimately required relying upon your business construction and area.

Substance Name safeguards you at a state level

Brand name safeguards you at a government level

Carrying on with work as (a DBA) doesn't give legitimate security, however, it very well may be lawfully required

Area name safeguards your business site address

Every one of these name enrollments is lawfully free. Most independent companies attempt to involve a similar name for every sort of enrollment, yet you're not ordinarily expected to.

FOUR UNIQUE WAYS OF ENLISTING YOUR BUSINESS NAME

1. Substance or entity name

A substance name can safeguard the name of your business at a state level. Contingent upon your business construction and area, the state might expect you to enroll a lawful substance name. Your substance name is the way the state distinguishes your business. Each state might have various guidelines about what your substance name can be and the utilization of organization additions. Most states don't permit you to enroll a name that is as of now been enlisted by another person, and a few states require your element name to mirror the sort of business it addresses. As a rule, your substance name enlistment safeguards your business and forestalls any other person in the state from working under a similar element name. Be that as it may, there are exemptions relating to state and business structure.

Check with your state for rules about how to enroll your business name.

2. Brand name (Trademark)

A brand name can safeguard the name of your business, products, and administrations at a public level. Brand names forestall others in the equivalent (or comparable) industry in the US from utilizing your reserved names.

For instance, if you were a gadgets organization and needed to call your business Springfield Electronic Embellishments and one of your items Screen Cover 5000, reserving those names would forestall other hardware organizations or comparative items from utilizing those equivalent names. Organizations in each state are liable to reserve encroachment claims, which can demonstrate exorbitantly. That is the reason you ought to look at your forthcoming business, item, and administration names against the authority brand name data set, kept up with by the US Patent and Brand name Office.

3. Carrying on with work as (DBA) name

You could have to enlist your DBA — otherwise called a business trademark, made-up name, or expected name — with the state, province, or city your business is situated. Enlisting your DBA name doesn't give legitimate insurance without anyone else, however, most states expect you to enroll your DBA assuming you utilize one. Some business structures expect you to utilize a DBA. At any rate, regardless of whether you're not expected to enlist a DBA, you could need to. A DBA allows you to lead a business under an alternate character from your very own name or your proper business substance name. To sweeten the deal, getting a DBA and government charge ID number (EIN) permits you to start a business ledger. Different organizations can go by a similar DBA in one state, so you're less confined in what you can pick. There's additionally more room in the lucidity of business capability. For instance, an entrepreneur could involve Springfield Electronic Frill for their substance name but use TechBuddy for their DBA. Simply recollect that brand name encroachment regulations will in any case apply.

Decide your DBA necessities in light of your particular area. Prerequisites change by business structure as well as by state, region, and district, so check with neighborhood government workplaces and sites.

4. Domain name

If you need a web-based presence for your business, begin by enlisting a space name — otherwise called your site address, or URL.

When you register your space name, no other person can utilize it however long you keep on possessing it. It's an effective method for safeguarding your image presence on the web. If another person has proactively enlisted the space you needed to utilize, that is completely fine. Your area name shouldn't be equivalent to your legitimate business name, brand name, or DBA. For instance, Springfield Electronic Embellishments could enroll the space name techbuddyspringfield.com. You'll enlist your space name through a recorder administration. Counsel an index of certified enlistment centers to figure out which ones are protected to utilize, and afterward, pick one that offers you the best blend of cost and client support. You'll have to restore your space enrollment consistently.

See whether you want to register your business

Your area and business structure decide how you'll have to enlist your business. Decide those elements first, and enlistment turns out to be extremely clear. For most independent ventures, enlisting your business is all around as basic as enrolling your business name with state and neighborhood legislatures. At times, you don't have to enroll by any stretch of the imagination. If you lead a business as yourself utilizing your legitimate name, you won't have to enroll anyplace. Be that as it may, recall, on the off chance that you don't enroll your business, you could pass up private risk insurance, legitimate advantages, and tax cuts.

Register with government organizations

Most organizations don't have to enroll with the national government to turn into a legitimate substance, other than essentially documenting to get a bureaucratic expense ID. Private ventures in some cases register with the central government for brand name assurance or duty-absolved status. If you have any desire to reserve your business, image, or item name, record with the US Patent and Brand name office whenever you've framed your business.

If you need charge excluded status for a charitable company, register your business as a duty-excluded substance with the IRS.

Register with state organizations

If your business is a limited liability company (LLC), company, association, or charitable enterprise, you'll most likely need to enlist with any state where you lead business exercises.

Ordinarily, you're viewed as directing business exercises in a state when:

- Your business has an actual presence in the state
- You frequently have face-to-face gatherings with clients in the state
- A huge part of your organization's income comes from the state
- Any of your representatives work in the state

A few states permit you to enlist on the web, and a few states make you record paper reports face-to-face or through the mail. Most states expect you to enroll with the Secretary of State's office, a Business Department, or a Business Organization.

Get an enrolled specialist

If your business is an LLC, company, association, or philanthropic partnership, you'll require an enrolled specialist in your state before you record. An enlisted specialist gets official papers and authoritative reports in the interest of your organization. The enrolled specialist should be situated in the state where you register. Numerous entrepreneurs like to utilize an enlisted specialist administration as opposed to taking on this job themselves.

File for foreign qualification

If your LLC, company, association, or philanthropic partnership conducts business exercises in more than one state, you could have to frame your business in one state and afterward record for unfamiliar capability in different states where your business is dynamic. The state where you structure your business will believe your business to be homegrown, while each other state will see your business as unfamiliar. Unfamiliar capability tells the express that an unfamiliar business is dynamic there. Unfamiliar qualified organizations normally need to cover charges and yearly report expenses in both their condition of arrangement and states where they're unfamiliar qualified. To unfamiliar qualify, document a Testament of Power with the state. Many states likewise require an Endorsement of Good Remaining from your condition of development. Each state charges a documenting expense, yet the sum fluctuates by state and business structure.

Look at state workplaces to track down unfamiliar capability necessities and charges.

File state archives and charges

As a rule, the complete expense to enroll your business will be under $300, however, charges change contingent upon your state and business structure.

The data you'll require commonly incorporates:

- Business name
- Business area
- Proprietorship, the board construction, or chiefs
- Enlisted specialist data
- Number and worth of offers (on the off chance that you're an enterprise)

The archives you want — and what goes in them — will differ in light of your state and business structure.

7. REGISTER YOUR BUSINESS

Whenever you've picked the ideal business name, now is the right time to make it lawful and safeguard your image. On the off chance that you're carrying on with work under a name unique to your own, you'll have to enroll with the national government, and perhaps your state government, as well.

See whether you want to enroll your business

Your area and business structure decide how you'll have to enroll your business. Decide those variables first, and enlistment turns out to be exceptionally direct. For most private companies, enlisting your business is all around as basic as enrolling your business name with state and neighborhood legislatures. At times, you don't have to enlist by any means. If you lead a business as yourself utilizing your legitimate name, you won't have to enroll anyplace. Be that as it may, recall, if you don't enroll your business, you could pass up private responsibility security, lawful advantages, and tax breaks. Most organizations don't have to enroll with the national government to turn into a legitimate substance, other than just documenting to get a bureaucratic expense ID. Private ventures some of the time register with the central government for brand name insurance or assessment excluded status. To reserve your business, image, or item name, document with the US Patent and Brand name office whenever you've framed your business.

If you need to charge excluded status for a charitable company, register your business as a duty-absolved element with the IRS.

Business enlistment records shipped off nearby, state, and government organizations.

Register with state offices

On the off chance that your business is a limited liability company (LLC), company, association, or not-for-profit enterprise, you'll most likely need to enroll with any state where you direct business exercises.

Ordinarily, you're viewed as directing business exercises in a state when:

- ✓ Your business has an actual presence in the state
- ✓ You frequently have face-to-face gatherings with clients in the state
- ✓ A huge part of your organization's income comes from the state
- ✓ Any of your representatives work in the state

A few states permit you to enroll on the web, and a few states make you record paper reports face-to-face or through the mail. Most states expect you to enlist with the Secretary of State's office, a Business Department, or a Business Office.

Document for unfamiliar capability

If your LLC, enterprise, association, or charitable partnership conducts business exercises in more than one state, you could have to shape your business in one state and afterward document for unfamiliar capability in different states where your business is dynamic. The state where you structure your business will believe your business to be homegrown, while each other state will see your business as unfamiliar. Unfamiliar capability informs the express that an unfamiliar business is dynamic there. Unfamiliar qualified organizations regularly need to settle charges and yearly report expenses in both their condition of arrangement and states where they're unfamiliar qualified. To unfamiliar qualify, document a Testament of Power with the state. Many states likewise require a Testament of Good Remaining from your condition of development. Each state charges a documenting expense, yet the sum shifts by state and business structure.

Look at state workplaces to track down unfamiliar capability prerequisites and expenses.

Record state archives and expenses

Much of the time, the all-out cost to enlist your business will be under $300, however, expenses shift contingent upon your state and business structure.

The data you'll require normally incorporates:

- ★ Business name
- ★ Business area
- ★ Proprietorship, the board design, or chiefs
- ★ Enlisted specialist data

Number and worth of offers (on the off chance that you're a company)

The records you want — and what goes in them — will fluctuate given your state and business structure.

Register with nearby organizations

Commonly, you don't have to enroll with area or regional authorities to frame your business. Assuming your business is an LLC, enterprise, association, or charitable partnership, you could have to petition for licenses and allows from the province or city. A few provinces and urban communities likewise expect you to enlist your DBA — a trademark or an imaginary name — if you utilize one. Neighborhood state-run administrations decide enrollment, authorizing, and allowing prerequisites, so visit nearby government sites to figure out what you want to do.

Keep awake to date with enlistment necessities

A few states expect you to give reports not long after enrolling relying upon your business structure. You might have to record extra documentation with your state charge board or establishment charge board. These filings are normally alluded to as Starting Reports or Expense Board enrollment, and most frequently should be documented within 30-90 days after you register with the state.

Check with your nearby duty office or establishment charge board, assuming it concerns you.

8. GET FEDERAL AND STATE TAX IDS

You'll utilize your employer's identification number (EIN) for significant stages to begin and develop your business, such as opening a ledger and making good on charges. It resembles a government-backed retirement number for your business. Some — however not all — states expect you to get a duty ID too.

Your state charge ID and government charge ID numbers — otherwise called an employer's identification Number (EIN) — work like an individual federal retirement aide number, yet for your business. They let your private company pay state and government charges. Your Boss ID Number (EIN) is your government-charge ID. You want it to cover government charges, enlist workers, open a ledger, and apply for permits to operate and allow.

It's allowed to apply for an EIN, and you ought to get it done just after you register your business.

Your business needs a government charge ID number if it does any of the accompanyings:

Pays workers

Works as a company of organization

Documents expense forms for work, extract, or liquor, tobacco, and guns

Keeps charges on pay, other than compensation, paid to a non-inhabitant outsider

Utilizes a Keogh Plan (an expense-conceded benefits plan)

Works with specific sorts of associations

Apply for an EIN with the IRS help device. It will direct you through questions and request your name, federal retirement aide number, address, and your "carrying on with work as" (DBA) name. Your nine-digit government charge ID opens up promptly upon confirmation.

Change or supplant your EIN

Assuming you as of now have an EIN, you could need to change or supplant it with another one if specific changes have happened with your business, contingent upon your business structure and the sort of progress that happened. Check with the IRS to decide precisely whether you want to change or supplant your EIN.

Get a state charge ID number

The requirement for a state charge ID number ties straightforwardly to whether your business should make good on state charges. In some cases, you can involve state charge ID numbers for different capabilities, similar to security against wholesale fraud for sole owners. Charge commitments contrast at the state and neighborhood levels, so you'll have to check with your state's sites. To know whether you want a state charge ID, research and comprehend your state's regulations regarding personal expenses and work burdens, the two most normal types of state charges for private ventures.

The interaction to get a state charge ID number is like getting a government charge ID number, yet it will change by state. You'll need to check with your state government for explicit advances.

State pay and work charges for organizations

Seven states have no annual duty, and another two just force charges on pay from profits. States that in all actuality burden pay will decide figures in light of business structure. Burdens likewise change by the state on business protection and laborers' remuneration protection. Comprehend these and different ramifications in computing startup costs and picking a business structure.

Visit your state's site to recognize whether you want to set a state charge ID number up to make good on state charges.

9. APPLY FOR LICENSES AND PERMITS

Keep your business chugging along as expected by remaining legitimately agreeable. The licenses and allows you want for your business will change by industry, state, area, and different variables.

Federal licenses and permits

You'll have to get a government permit or grant on the off chance that your business exercises are controlled by a bureaucratic office.

State licenses and permits

The licenses and allows you want from the state, province, or city will rely upon your business exercises and business area. Your permit to operate expenses will likewise shift. States will generally control a more extensive scope of exercises than the central government. For instance, business exercises that are normally controlled locally incorporate sell-offs, development, cleaning, cultivating, plumbing, eateries, retail, and candy machines. A few licenses allow lapse after a set timeframe. Monitor when you want to restore them — it's frequently simpler to reestablish than it is to apply for another one. You'll need to explore your state, district, and city guidelines. Industry prerequisites frequently fluctuate by state. Visit your state's site to figure out which allows and licenses you to want.

10. OPEN A BUSINESS BANK ACCOUNT

An independent venture financial records can assist you with taking care of lawful, expense, and everyday issues. The uplifting news is it's not difficult to set one up assuming you have the right enrollments and desk work prepared.

Advantages of business bank account

When you begin tolerating or burning cash as your business, you ought to start a business ledger. Normal business accounts incorporate financial records, bank accounts, Mastercard accounts, and dealer administrations account. Dealer administration accounts permit you to acknowledge credit and check card exchanges from your clients.

You can start a business financial balance whenever you've got your government EIN.

Most business ledgers offer advantages that don't accompany a standard individual financial balance.

Security. Business banking offers restricted individual risk insurance by keeping your business finances separate from your assets. Dealer benefits additionally offer buy assurance for your clients and guarantee that their data is secure. Impressive skill. Clients will want to pay you with charge cards and make looks at your business rather than straightforwardly to you. Additionally, you'll have the option to approve representatives to deal with everyday financial errands for the benefit of the business. Readiness. Business banking ordinarily accompanies the choice for a credit extension for the organization. This can be utilized in case of a crisis, or on the other hand assuming your business needs new hardware. Buying power. Visa records can assist your business with making huge startup buys and assist with laying out a financial record for your business.

Track down a record with low expenses and great advantages

Some entrepreneurs open a business account at a similar bank they use for their records. Rates, charges, and choices shift from one bank to another, so you ought to look around to ensure you track down the most reduced expenses and the best advantages.

Here are interesting points while you're starting a business checking or bank account:

- Early on offers
- Loan fees for investment funds and checking
- Loan fees for credit extensions
- Exchange charges
- Contractually allowable charges
- Least record balance charges

Here are interesting points while you're opening a shipper administrations account:

Rebate rate: The rate charged for each exchange handled

Exchange expenses: The sum charged for each Visa exchange

Address verification service (AVS) charges

ACH day-to-day bunch expenses: Expenses charged when you settle Mastercard exchanges for that day

Month-to-month lease expenses: Expenses charged if your business doesn't meet the base required exchanges

Installment handling organizations are an inexorably well-known option in contrast to conventional trader administration accounts. Installment handling organizations at times give additional usefulness, similar to frills that let you utilize your telephone to acknowledge charge card installments. The charge classes that you want to consider will be like dealer administrations account expenses. If you track down an installment processor that you like, recall that you'll in any case have to interface it to a business financial records to get installments.

Get documents if you really want to start a business bank account.

Starting a business bank account is simple whenever you've picked your bank. Just go on the web or to a nearby office to start the cycle. Here are probably the most well-known reports banks request when you open a business financial balance. A few banks might request more.

www.ingramcontent.com/pod-product-compliance
Lightning Source LLC
Chambersburg PA
CBHW070318220526
45465CB00004B/1900